G000150104

JEAN-PAUL HÉVIN®

CHOCOLATIER

PARIS

© 2008 Assouline Publishing
601 West 26th Street, 18th Floor
New York, NY 10001, USA
Tel.: 212 989-6769 Fax: 212 647-0005
www.assouline.com

Translated from the French by Nancy Dunham

Color separation: Planète Couleurs (France)

Printed in China

ISBN: 978 2 7594 0257 1

10 9 8 7 6 5 4 3 2

JEAN-PAUL HÉVIN®

CHOCOLATIER

PARIS

FRANÇOIS SIMON

ASSOULINE

The taste of childhood

it seems that dull environments sometimes can inspire greatness, acting as a foil against which a select few labor. While some locales attract, fascinate, sublimate, beautify, or quite simply heal, there are others whose soporific dimension can be a real gift in disguise. In literature, film, gastronomy, and music, examples abound of destinies exacerbated by a native city that was indolent, insipid, and nondescript. Many Belgian surrealists exhibited flashes of brilliance as a result of living in a country that was deceptively flat; Châteauroux and its provincial indifference was a veritable catharsis for the actor Gérard Depardieu; the city of Laval was no doubt the cause for the impatience of a young child named Alfred Jarry, who would become a forerunner to the Surrealist movement. So according to this gentle logic, it is reasonable to think that Jean-Paul Hévin, after a happy childhood in the pleasant town of Méral, France, on the outer edge of Haut-Anjou in the Mayenne region, probably felt an itch to move on.

It would be easy to spend ten or so years in this village, set on the border of the area called Bas-Maine, near the boundary with Brittany, watching the Oudon river flowing past at its own lethargic rhythm. Then one day you might awaken and ask yourself what you will become. Jean-Paul Hévin lived with his loving parents in this countryside. His father was an arboriculturalist, meaning he grew fruit trees. They were everywhere on the farm: cherry trees, plum trees, pear trees, mirabelles, nectarines—all there for the picking. Like everyone on the farm, Jean-Paul's mother had daily chores to attend to, such as taking care of the house, the cows, goats, horses, chickens, geese, ducks, and dogs. You could spend a lifetime there, and, in fact, the elder Hévins did. Sometimes, the family didn't even bother to change their clocks to daylight savings time.

Jean-Paul Hévin adored this life, with its serene rhythms. But a feeling of well-being can be pernicious. When you're an adolescent, people ask you what you want to become: You search confusedly in your store of images; you say the first thing that pops into your head. Jean-Paul's answer: He would be an electronics specialist. That was acceptable, there were job openings. At the time, it was a real profession for a studious and resourceful boy. And, by chance, there was a *lycée technique* (technical school) in the city of Laval. Jean-Paul Hévin's future was all laid out.

Just as some cities or circumstances awaken the spirit, there is also a category (just as long) for the awakenings that do not occur. You avoid a plane crash, the departure of a train to the wrong destination, and you receive other unexpected gifts. Jean-Paul Hévin forgot to register at the technical school.

As a result, he was hurriedly admitted to a vocational school for confectioners and pastry chefs. After all, the young man loved pastry. Even today, he recalls the sweet traces of his future profession: fruits everywhere, including the kitchen. The first pie he made to please his mother was apple. It was sufficient basis for a career. The foundations were solid: He already possessed full, active senses and a gentleness of spirit; the technique would not be far behind. It had to bake in the oven a few years, rise slowly; then the steaming door could be opened.

Jean-Paul Hévin doesn't talk much of those early years. Modesty, no doubt. Especially since he is a reserved man. What's the good of talking, explaining, or of coloring a story? For Hévin, a few dates are enough, an emphatic look. The attitude reflects his upbringing. In Mayenne, discretion comes naturally. Soccer is played with moderation, no furious kicks; kitchens simmer quietly. Ferraris never honk beside the café terraces, chefs never wear their hats backward, words are never spoken loudly. Hévin's adolescence was like so many others.

In his view, it's nothing to make a fuss about. You already know enough. Besides, if he did talk about it, it would be tender, peaceful, milky—like the landscapes of these serene regions. His childhood exuded a feeling not of slowness, but of a steady rhythm. In memory, even the rivers seem to stand still. Meals consist of white meats, blond pies, and golden sugar. Nevertheless, there comes a time when things are set in motion. Was it like Newton's apple or a slap on the forehead? No. At most, we might retrieve from memory the Sunday cakes. It's a shared memory: chocolate cream puffs, coffee-flavored éclairs, paris-brests, saint-honorés, meringues…Sweet heaven! The smell of Sundays, those endless days, the gentle discouragement of flavorless afternoons, the neurasthenia of the country. This is also how impatience begins, how you suddenly find yourself filled with exasperation, that divine muscle. In fact, it is this taste of childhood that intricately forms you with its flavors: the bitter, acid, sweet, and salty—and, of course, the spicy! This taste follows you in life, though you might seem to forget it. But already the paths are emerging. One apple pie does not make a pastry chef: There is much to learn beyond the taste of childhood.

The taste for learning

Vocational schools often possess a certain sadness. To feel that strange melancholy, it's enough to walk through the provincial cities when the students are just getting out of class. Very often these students attend such schools because of idleness, offhandedness, or disenchantment. Not that they feel excluded, but society has already sent them a signal. They will not go to the important classes, schools, or universities. Frequently, this signal is taken as an insult. It leaves a bitter taste. But bitterness is not necessarily an unpleasant taste. Bitterness can be a strange tool: When it is handled in the right way, it can lift destinies like it lifts many great dishes. For example, there could be no *lièvre* (hare) *à la royale* without a touch of bitterness, thanks to chocolate—chocolate? How surprising!

There are schools that appreciate this kind of paradox, such as the Robert Buron vocational school in Laval. Indeed, it takes just one or two charismatic professors to light the spark. After all, there are surely less rewarding fates than watching soufflés rise (even those flavored with Grand Marnier) and chantilly creams blossom, than filling éclairs, making *pièces montées* (decorative confectionary centerpieces), or sprinkling icing sugar like frost in November.

Confectioners' schools do sometimes have a major flaw: They venerate technique and effect solely for the sake of technique and effect. Often, pallid students come to contests to display white chocolate swans, French armoires made from dark chocolate, steeples of spun sugar.

The world of pastry similarly encompasses its own sort of kitsch, pretty but disarming. We could bemoan these facts, but we are reminded of those cities and circumstances that we spoke of earlier. Suddenly, desire arrives like a shot of adrenaline: Escape from these white chocolate/dark chocolate balloons, these Tyrolean chalets with angelica lawns, these candied cherries on the top of the cake. Jean-Paul Hévin knows this world by heart. He does not talk of it, either through charity or through indifference. After all, we make it through the rain not with words but with action.

Jean-Paul Hévin had his own years of contests and medals (though not in chocolate). He saw and tried it all: gold medal in Arpajon, 1979; Charles Proust award, 1980; French National Pastry Cup, 1983; first prize in the Grand Prix International de la Chocolaterie, 1983; Vase de Sèvres in Arpajon, 1984, awarded by the French president at the time, François Mitterrand. That's why today, he knows where he's coming from and where he's heading. He saw the profession of pastry chef weighed down by a dated aesthetic (tacky, to be precise), latent poor taste (the great paradox of gastronomy haunted by taste and the search for excellence), and an atmosphere of suffering born under neon lights and kitchen vapors.

Jean-Paul Hévin quickly understood that the world of pastry was a world of the excluded, a continuation of the vocational school.

In the kitchen, there are three categories of people: chefs, pastry chefs, and dishwashers. When chefs are asked about their staff, that is invariably their response. It's how the savory chefs get their revenge on life: for a long time, they were the renegades of the table, held in check by the superb and arrogant service in the front of the house. It wasn't until journalists Henri Gault and Christian Millau championed nouvelle cuisine in the 1960s and 1970s that chefs became popular. Suddenly, we saw them step out of their kitchens, we saw their photographs in magazines, and we even heard them lecture.

Since then, the adoration of the chef hasn't stopped: The bell of change has been rung, and for a long time now the whipping boys have been the pastry chefs. When dessert arrives (and this is often obvious at many tables), diners have lost their appetite—the savory chefs have ruined it by stuffing their patrons full. This is what Jean-Paul Hévin's whole generation had to fight against. They had to learn to overcome ingratitude for their gifts.

but life has not been unfair to Jean-Paul Hévin: as part of a tightly packed and exciting professional path, he joined the Hotel Nikko, in 1976. He was then nineteen years old. One of the greatest chefs in the world worked there: Joël Robuchon.

Robuchon already had a terrible reputation. Stories circulated of a chef draconian to the point of tyranny. But many of the older crowd, including chef Thierry Marx, believe that it was a false reputation. People often put pressure on themselves. "They wanted to make me out to be an executioner," Robuchon responds. "I am demanding.

I like rigor, cleanliness, discipline." Joël Robuchon forgot to mention one thing that Jean-Paul Hévin would discover and interiorize: speed.

You have to see the service in a large restaurant to realize the formidable speed of Jean-Paul Hévin's profession. At noon, everything is impressively calm, but the storm is not long in coming. The cooks manifest a motionless intensity. They know that, in an instant, all hell will break loose, but they never know from where. Perhaps thirty minutes later, the orders arrive like the customers —together.

The kitchen is bombarded from all sides. There isn't even time for a chef to fly into a rage. If he or she does, it is often extremely violent and incredibly swift—a sort of white rage that consumes all. It goes with the territory.

For hours, the chefs, cooks, and runners all must play at being Hindu gods, throwing plates in all directions. As a pastry chef Jean-Paul Hévin learned this haste and adapted to it.

In this setting, Jean-Paul Hévin inevitably had to enter the contest for the Meilleur Ouvrier de France (best craft worker in France). It was in 1986: He presented a nut and chestnut composition. This contest is considered the profession's supreme prize. When you ask the greatest chefs what they regard as the proudest moment in their career, they sometimes mention the number of stars they've been awarded, but they also always mention the title of Meilleur Ouvrier de France. It is a chef's greatest honor.

Why? Like Jean-Paul Hévin, the award winners often remain silent on the subject. Perhaps it is indescribable.

The taste of Japan

i t was at this same time that Jean-Paul Hévin discovered Japan. Through a combination of circumstances not unusual in the profession, Jean-Paul Hévin departed for the Land of the Rising Sun practically overnight. With such opportunities, you don't have time to think. In the world of gastronomy, you may be called one Friday afternoon. Monday morning, you arrive, suffering from jetlag, at Tokyo's Narita International Airport. A car comes for you. The next morning, you enter the depths of a pastry shop. No one, including Hévin, ever comes out the same. He emerged newly alive and incredibly changed. This experience propelled Jean-Paul Hévin into a new life.

At the time, Japan was discovering the world of Western flavors. It was also experiencing an incredible economic and financial success in those years, called the "bubble" years: With phenomenal poise and speed, the archipelago would take the gastronomical world by storm—with passion, humility, and an unparalleled thirst for knowledge. Where other countries held back, Japan charged ahead. Where there was a master, Japan climbed on that master's shoulders. After twenty years of learning and observation, Japan today ranks as one of the best connoisseur countries in the world. It's easy to find exceptional croissants even in remote corners of Japan.

Jean-Paul Hévin landed in a country that didn't know him, although he knew it and was already breathing in its culture. He became manager of a branch of the famous, though now-defunct, Parisian pastry shop Peltier, but his staff went about their own business and kept to themselves. Was he in charge of the shop, or only of himself? For two years, he would "endure," in order to understand this country that would give him much in exchange. He tried to be like others—as you do in Japan—to better understand them. He would not mimic but assimilate, become a chameleon. On weekends he traveled, disappearing to Japan's far reaches, even to the islands. He would lose himself, then return with the same fever.

After Laval and Paris, Japan was Jean-Paul's third voyage of initiation. He submerged himself in Japanese culture, learned to speak Japanese, and became an enthusiast of photography, Kabuki (traditional Japanese theater), and karate. Of course, he also practiced his profession. He traced the life of a square of chocolate step-by-step: It has thirty days ahead of it—including eight days in the shop and fifteen at the customer's home. He had to play it short and sweet. Like he does today, Jean-Paul Hévin spent his days and nights probing the secrets of chocolate. It was a kind of obsessive research. Hévin knew he could always do better, and he aimed for the ultimate level of knowledge and skill. For him, good was the enemy of better. To go further, that was the credo he learned in Japan.

Presently, Jean-Paul Hévin owns more than five shops in Japan: in Hakata, Hiroshima, Kokura and Tokyo (Omotesando, Roppongi and Shinjuku) . . . He participates in televised shows, and his deluxe hot chocolate once sparked an extraordinary craze—during its launch, people lined up for more than three hours to taste this exhilarating preparation. At Tokyo's Salon du Chocolat in January 2007, fourteen thousand visitors flocked to the Isetan department store in just two days to see the creations of the man some did not hesitate to call "a living masterpiece."

Japan celebrated him and, whether in the Isetan stores or elsewhere, Japanese chocolatiers even managed to catch up to the chocolate master. Better still, the Japanese drove Jean-Paul Hévin into a corner. He worked at combinations that would have made French blood boil: chocolate stuffed with. . . cheese, or the art of marrying it to Epoisses,

Roquefort, and Livarot. Jean-Paul Hévin was in demand everywhere: In 2002, he began hosting a cooking show on the Japanese station NHK; he signed autographs; and he was greeted as he stepped off planes. He was delighted to find a country totally free of complexes regarding culinary habits, one that was open to excellence, humble in learning, and especially respectful of skillfully crafted work.

In Japan, Hévin learned all sorts of nuances, sensorial diagrams. He realized that the Japanese were taking great steps forward, accepting notions that to the French had seemed familiar for centuries: strong aromas (in cheeses, wines, and game), the crunchiness of bread (as opposed to the soft, sticky, spongy textures in Japan). He discovered that the present and the past cohabit in a surprising way. "I am not one of those who criticize the Japanese for having built an ultramodern Tokyo," wrote Henri Michaux, "to have filled it with cafés, styled like decorative art exhibits (Tokyo is a hundred thousand times more modern than Paris). To have adopted clean and pure geometry in furnishings and decoration. We could criticize the French for being modern, not the Japanese. The Japanese have been modern for a thousand years. Nowhere in Japan do we find even the smallest trace of those stupid pretensions in what we called the Louis XV style, the Directoire, the Empire style, etc."

1 ike any foreigner plunged into Japanese life, Jean-Paul Hévin would unlearn to better understand. He discovered notions that have fallen out of use in the West, such as blandness, a shadow that Japanese writer Junichiro Tanizaki praised highly. What did he say? "The 'mysterious Orient' of which Westerners speak probably refers to the uncanny silence of these shadows [...].

We Orientals create beauty by creating shadows in places that are in themselves insignificant [...]. Japanese cooking, if it is served in overly bright rooms, on predominantly white dishes, loses half of its appeal." We find this shadow, too, in boxes of chocolate, with the varying colors—soft, deep, powdery—paralleling the mysterious colors of the night. Hévin discovered notions such as *koi* (romantic love). While in Japan, Jean-Paul Hévin took his philosophy of chocolate to new limits: he looked inward, built a passion based not on Western-style love (*ai*), but on an addiction of the senses.

Jean-Paul Hévin would return from Japan with a greater attention to the smallest detail and a sort-of drunken delight found in the proximity of his creations one to another. To learn to look and to live each instant creates a sort of 360° vision that ought to be our daily lot. This conscious way of looking accompanies the cooking of chocolate, its preparations, and the choice of beans. One places oneself in the position of "omniscient spectator" (comparable to the lessons of the Actor's Studio, where actors must totally possess their role and penetrate their subject, even an object, to the point of giving the impression of being, say, a chair). It is the work of a voyeur, a kind of chocolaty schizophrenia, as if suddenly you had lifted the lid off of chocolate to plunge into its cavalier perspectives. Chocolate and the art of its cooking are composed of many influences and contain multiple parameters. All the details remain essential and must be mastered.

In this vertiginous game, you quickly see that all is connected and all corresponds. "Everything is implied," wrote the Swiss travel writer Nicolas Bouvier, "related, attributed, placed under the patronage of a famous person or shadow, and every peony bush catches you in ignorance." In Japan, Jean-Paul Hévin found consistency in precision: it wandered from karate movements to the shape of a chocolate.

The taste of chocolate

Wiser for this trip to Japan, Jean-Paul Hévin would take his passion for chocolate to new heights. His return to France would be marked by the same vigilant vivacity. At twenty-nine years of age, he bought the shop Le Petit Boulé, at 16 avenue de la Motte-Piquet in Paris' seventh arrondissement. Why *petit boulé* (little ball)? It was simply a nod to the life of sugar. Sugar goes through several stages when it is cooked: the "thread" stage (103°C –105°C or 217°F–221°F), ideal for almond paste; the "pearl" stage (110°C–112°C or 230°F–233°F) when bubbles start to form; the "soft-ball" stage (119°C–123°C or 246°F–253°F) when the syrup has thickened and in water forms a soft malleable ball, ideal for fondant and frosted fruits; the "firm to hard-ball" stage (126°C–135°C or 258°F– 275°F), before the sugar enters another sphere; and the "soft-crack" stage (145°C–150°C or 290°F–302°F) with its happy cohort of lollipops, hard toffees, and cotton candy.

Passionate, exhilarated by work both night and day, Hévin entered the intriguing whirl of effort pushed to its limits, as though he was passing through a looking glass to get to a truth. He did it with the serenity of those who return from uninhabited lands. You have to see Jean-Paul Hévin like this, tasting a chocolate, to realize the well-being that dwells in him: He takes it delicately between his fingers and slips it into his mouth—he warms it. It's a method for tasting chocolate that Hévin savors and one for you to try.

When Hévin tastes chocolate, it's as though he were receiving communion, his whole being unfurls its antenna, analyzes, and savors. His face lights up; he is strangely possessed, as if he and the chocolate were one and the same, as if he were taking religious vows.

This search for the truth about chocolate takes him to Brazil, seeking special beans. He travels, visits, inhales, and compares. He seeks criollo beans in Venezuela and Colombia. We may find him in Caracas, like a James Bond of the chocolate block, in Madagascar, in Ecuador. Or perhaps he has already moved on, probably far from his traditional menu of fifty chocolate creations, including Safi cakes with cacao almond biscuit, chocolate, and bitter orange mousse; or Bergam with ganache biscuit, praline pastry, milk chocolate, and bergamot mousse; chocolate bars from the woodsy Java to the soft and tender Trinité; ready-to-eat chocolate; or squares of coffee-flavored dark chocolate, of milk chocolate/praline pastry. There are never any symbols in the centrifugal sultriness of his creations but rather constant associations, ideas, and images for the person who wants to climb up on this magic palanquin.

today, in this other journey, Hévin seems to have found himself, to resemble his creations with his somber elegance (lots of black and anthracite) as though he had become that magic shadow.

Not for him, the foil wrappings: he's already somewhere else, like an impatient horse that stamps at the ground and then runs off.

Why are Jean-Paul Hévin's chocolates so elegant, their flavor so arousing? Because, he has entered deep into the dark heart of chocolate.

Chocolate Tart

Praline Longchamp

Praline Feuilletine

Safi

Choco Passion

Chocolate Millefeuille

Caracas

Ecuador

Turin

Bergam

Chocolate Raspberry

Cigar

-fashioned Macaroon

Marquise

Mont-Blanc

Guayaquil

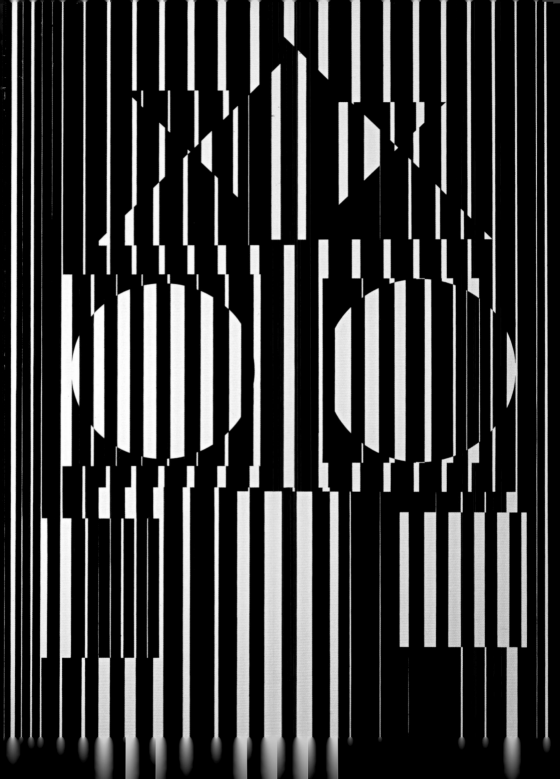

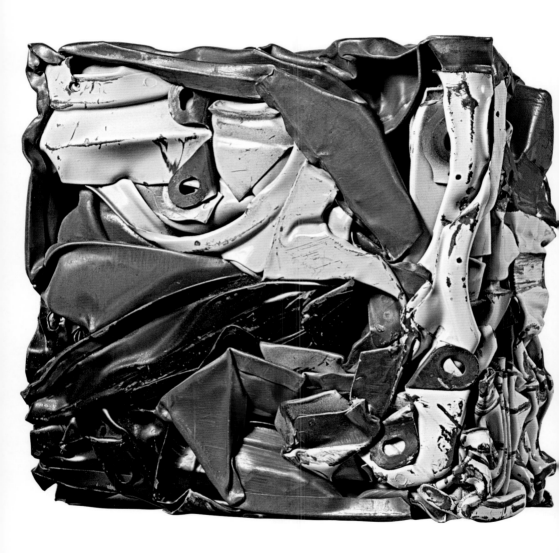

PRIERE DE TOUCHER

NOTRE ENQUÊTE
LES MEILLEURS ÉCLAIRS AU CHOCOLAT DE PARIS

CARMEN-PICASSO
LA CORRIDA DU DÉSIR

ANNA NETREBKO
DIVINE SOPRANO AU TCE

愛在巴黎

In the City of Love

巴黎人是浪漫的。巴黎人的浪漫，造就了這座城市的迷人姿態，再平凡簡單的場景事物，因為血液裡留著浪漫因子的巴黎人隨意的一舉一手一投足，頓時氣氛百分百，映入眼簾的一景一物也隨之沾染上美麗的色彩。TEXT · Niki DE LOOZE · Kang Wei PHOTO · Atgis Pudokas Kim

---

Le marché de JEAN-PAUL HE...

Après avoir séduit les spectateurs de l'émission "Chic" su le fameux chocolatier nous confie ses bonnes adresses.

Jean-Paul Hévin,
231, rue Saint-Honoré, 1er.

Excellent boucher (1) Je trouve ici du bœuf boutanei et de veau élevé sous la mère et je cuisine dans une cocotte en cuivre pour une cuisson accompagnés de petits légumes fricus et de pois paillasson. Mon truc : toujours jeter d'ail dans le panier du réfrigérateur lequel je trouve des morceaux de chou.
Barone, 6, rue de Marché-Saint-Honoré, 1er.

Boulanger préféré (2) J'aime sa baguette tradition. Sa saveur légèrement sucrée accompagne à merveille le saumon gravlax que je propose à midi dans mon salon de thé. Sublime aussi avec du beurre et un morceau de chocolat à 75 % de cacao provenant de São Tomé et Principe. Mon péché ? Une généreuse tranche recouverte de ma pâte à tartiner au praliné.
Boulanger Julien, 85, rue Saint-Dominique, 7e.

Mon épicerie du monde (3) Les épices et le chocolat se marient très bien. Ici, je trouve mon inspiration. J'y ai découvert le monde poivre (fleur de la noix de muscade), qui m'a servi pour une base au bonbon de chocolat Minuit. Pour mes ganaches, j'utilise volontiers du poivre de Sichuan, de la vanille et de la cannelle. Pour mon cake au chocolat, je prends de l'anis étoilé, de la graine de coriandre, de la muscade et du gingembre. Puis je mélange le tout, non pas à du chocolat mais à du cacao en poudre ! *Izraël, 30, rue François-Miron, 4e.*

Mon fournisseur de thés (4) J'aime que le thé soit préparé dans les règles de l'art. Mon pré-

féré : le Lapsang Souchong, un dans l'une de mes ganaches au g noncé, le Gemme. J'en bois to née ! Parmi mes découvertes : un thé fermenté chinois intestins let pour la digestion, que je ne te
Mariage Frères, 30, rue du Bourg-Tibou.

Mon maître fromager (5) Ce meilleu France 2000 n'hésite pas à réal ses créations, comme le brie de B en 2004, sous avons associé ses mes chocolats. Le résultat était s de l'étivag) à ajouté du miel de no noisettes et des morceaux de choc nilé-et-Tobago 75 %, choisi pour s Avec la mimolette 3 ans d'âge, j du cacao en poudre et du piment qui font ressortir la saveur fruitée Une manière intéressante de décou colat ! *Marie Quatrehomme, 62, rue*

Mon meilleur stout (6) Cette épicerie grand choix de produits qui perm liser les recettes décrites dans mo ces de chocolat » (éd. Flammari réussit, je recommande le choco vanille-orange 56 % de cacao de W les chocolats à l'extra-amer 6 pour les gâteaux. On trouve ici un variété de fruits secs comme les am pagne que j'utilise dans mes fours pâte d'amande ou gianduja ; les de Turquie que j'aime juste enro colés ; les gingembres confits de chissants en petits morceaux sur Pour tous les confiseries-pâtisse
G. Detou, 58, rue Tiquetonne, Rue 2e.

PROPOS RECUEILLIS

✓ **Le goût des produits Herm** hauteur de sa créativité. ble pour l'Ispahan, un classique. rines Emotions ou Sensations, aussi pour le kouglof, le kouign-a fruits rouges ou les Montebello, de fruits pistache-framboise. Un

Pierre Hermé, 185, rue de Vaugirard, 6e.

Chocolat chaud
recette page suivante

Jean-Paul Hévin dans sa première boutique parisienne, avenue de la Motte-Picquet. Un rendez-vous pris du Club des croqueurs de chocolat.

Q uand on a du talent en barre, ce n'est pas étonnant de finir dans le chocolat. Première bonne idée de Jean-Paul Hévin ? Troquer un avenir incertain contre un CAP de pâtissier. La suite est un rêve. Toujours au sommet, Star à Tokyo, notre chocolatier a aussi gagné la Coupe de France de pâtisserie, intégré le club fermé des Meilleurs Ouvriers de Frances (M.O.F.) et... décroché le prix du Meilleur Macaron de Paris. Pour Jasmin, notre homme nous a concocté un show à sa manière, un chocolat show!

Tartelettes au chocolat

Pour 6 personnes
Pâte sucrée au chocolat
• 140 g de beurre mou • 1 œuf
• 90 g de sucre glace • 30 g de poudre d'amandes • 2 gouttes de vanille
• 1 pincée de sel • 230 g de farine
• 25 g de chocolat à 70 % haché et fondu

Crémeux pour garnir
• 25 cl de crème • 280 g de chocolat à 70 % haché • 2 œufs + 2 jaunes
• 70 g de beurre frais

Glaçage au chocolat
• 60 g de sucre • 60 g d'eau • 50 g de crème • 100 g de chocolat à 70 %

Finition au caramel
• 40 g de sucre • 5 ml d'eau froide • 30 g de crème fleurette • 10 g de beurre salé

1. Mélanger le beurre, le sucre, les amandes, l Ajouter l'œuf, chocolat. Form

Préchauffer le four à 170 °C et cuire à blanc (sans garniture) de 15 à 20 min selon la taille.

2. Faire bouillir la crème, hors du feu la verser sur le chocolat. Lisser le mélange et incorporer les œufs et les jaunes, puis ajouter le beurre. Mélanger. Couler dans les fonds de tarte précuits. Passer au four pendant 10 min à 170 °C. Bien refroidir.

UNE COUPE DE CH

Balayées les flûtes en cristal, has les verres à vodka, cet hiver, c'e ces coupes qu'il faudra boire l'a La forme vous rappelle quelque Normal, il s'agit du mythique ve Harcourt de Boccarat, revisité pa le chocolatier Jean-Paul Hévin. rempli de perles chocolatées, ma nous, on trouve qu'il fait une co champagne à croquer... CATHE

■ 38 € le coffret de trois verres. www.je...

Le macaron à l'épreuve du goût

A TABLE
Nous avons testé la version chocolatée de ce classique de la pâtisserie. Bilan mitigé.

ILS SONT PARTOUT. Les petits gâteaux ronds aux allures de soucoupes volantes ont envahi les pâtisseries, les grands magasins, la carte des desserts, voire le bouquet des fleuristes. Chics, ludiques, mignons, tout ronds, les macarons sont les nouveaux cadeaux gourmands. D'origine incertaine - ils seraient venus d'Italie -, ils ont gravi quatre à quatre l'échelle sociale. Biscuits populaires hier, ils se font aujourd'hui relooker par des créateurs dans les épiceries fines. Et pour alimenter le désir, il se décline sur tous les tons. Pas une semaine ne se passe sans qu'apparaisse un nouveau parfum. Réglisse, lavande, caramel au beurre salé, carotte, pâte de haricot rouge, huile d'olive, truffe blanche ou encore

foie gras... À tous les goûts ça marche. Soigneusement exposés dans les vitrines, traités (avec des gants, s'il vous plaît) comme des objets précieux, ils sont à prendre avec des pincettes.

Pour juger de la qualité d'un macaron, mieux vaut s'en tenir aux classiques. Le parfum chocolat reste dans le top 5 des ventes et laisse décoller le goût d'amande caractéristique de ce biscuit meringué. C'est donc la version canaotée du macaron petit format, dit macaron « gerbet », qui a été retenue pour la dégustation. Nos critères ? Une forme ronde et dodue, l'équilibre entre la coque et la garniture, et un bon goût de chocolat marié au parfum de l'amande. Au final, qu'il soit (ou non) au cacao, le secret d'un bon macaron se résume à une simple équation : fondant dedans, craquant dehors.

Enquête réalisée par
ALEXANDRA MICHOT, ALEXANDRA BARDINI, FLORIANE RAVARD et E. S.

Les petits gâteaux au cacao du chocolatier Jean-Paul Hévin n'ont remporté tous les suffrages. *I.-L. Couzinet/Le Figaro*

Des surgelés pas très craquants

Puisque certains pâtissiers congèlent une partie de leur production, pourquoi ne pas acheter directement ses macarons au rayon surgelés ? D'autant que ceux vendus chez Thiriet (5,85 € les douze), Picard (6 € les seize) ou Mono-

seignes ne les vendent qu'en assortiment (chocolat, vanille, café et autre framboise dans la même barquette.

Une fois isolé, le macaron chocolat de Thiriet manque cruellement de relief. Mais son bon goût de cho-

vaut un 9,5/20. Si la cou l'apparence du macaron, p chez Monop'a Gourmet, si du macaron se résume à u La garniture crémeuse, pe beurrée, ne comble pas l'a cacao et récolte un petit

Jean-Paul Hévin
ジャン＝ポール・エヴァン

今年6月表参道ヒルズに、日本における5軒目のブティックをオープン。本国フランスにおけるチョコレートの評価はもちろんだが、2005年に開催された2回「マカロンコンクール」でも、クラシック部門で第1位を獲得。

Pour ses ganaches, palets, truffes... le chocolatier n'hésite pas à voyager plusieurs fois par an à Madagascar, au Venezuela ou en Colombie pour sélectionner les meilleures fèves.

Divin Hévin

'est par le plus pur des hasards que Judith More, éditrice anglaise de passage rue Saint-Honoré, à Paris, tombe sur la vitrine de Jean-Paul Hévin. Elle entre par curiosité, goûte un chocolat, un deuxième, puis finit par craquer sur le rayon entier. Aussitôt, elle se met en tête de publier outre-Manche un livre de recettes avec celui qu'elle considère aujourd'hui... et après moult comparaisons, comme « le meilleur pâtissier chocolatier du monde », l'incarnation même du chic à la française ». Voilà comment *Chocolate Heaven by Jean-*

Paul Hévin – Paradis chocolaté – s'apprête à faire fondre les papilles britanniques. Avant de sortir en France chez Flammarion, en octobre 2005.

« C'est ainsi, les opportunités sont toujours venues à moi », raconte (vrai ou faux modeste ?) le chocolatier. Disons plutôt que son talent a aussi été le fruit de belles rencontres.

Aujourd'hui, à 47 ans, il est l'un des rares dans son métier à avoir trouvé le juste dosage entre qualité – il a été promu « 5 tablettes » (la note maximale) dans l'édition 2003 du *Guide du Club des croqueurs de chocolat* – et quantité, puisqu'il possède 8 boutiques entre Paris et le Japon, emploie 140 personnes et fabrique pas moins de 35 tonnes de chocolat par an.

Pour autant, la réussite de l'intéressé ne s'accommode pas du moule des clichés. Sil-

silhouette musclée – 1,75 mètre pour 78 kilos affinée par douze ans de karaté, ensemble noir Rykiel homme : ce dandy à l'élégance sobre est loin de l'image convenue de l'artisan au tablier barbouillé. Ne comptez pas non plus sur lui pour égrener ses souvenirs gourmands d'enfance, comme le font si facilement les grandes toques. Trop de pudeur. Tout juste a-t-on droit à quelques bribes impressionnistes sur sa jeunesse à Méral, en Mayenne, ses parents agriculteurs, son rêve d'une carrière dans l'électronique, contrarié « à cause d'une inscription ratée », et son CAP de pâtisserie à Laval, « sans trop y croire ». Et la passion du chocolat dans tout ça ? « Je m'y suis intéressé grâce à Joël Robuchon. En 1976, j'étais déjà chef pâtissier à l'hôtel Nikko quand il est arrivé aux fourneaux. Toutes les équipes sont parties du jour au lendemain, mais je lui ai dit que j'avais envie d'apprendre, alors il m'a gardé et c'est lui qui m'a vraiment initié aux subtilités du cacao. » Modèle de technicité, le chef côtoie la passion, insuffle aussi son goût quasi névrotique pour la performance. Pendant dix ans, il est coureur d'une « concourite » aiguë, qui l'amène d'ailleurs de médailles d'or en premiers prix, jusqu'à obtenir à plus gratifiante de toutes les récompenses à ses yeux, le titre de « meilleur ouvrier de France » en 1986. « Une finale où, comme un sportif de haut niveau, je me souviens d'avoir été véritablement en transe ! »

Fort de cette brassée de lauriers, il ouvre en 1988 sa première boutique parisienne, avenue de La Motte-Picquet, suivie, quelques mois plus tard, par une autre, rue Vavin. Totalement inconnu du grand public, il n'en a rien à faire, fort de sa clientèle de fidèles qui viennent croquer ici les créations

Certains parlent de lui comme du meilleur chocolatier au monde. A l'occasion des fêtes de Pâques, parcours et recettes exclusives de cet artisan qui réinvente le cacao

en Mayenne **1986** meilleur ouvrier de France **1988** ouverture de sa première

STAGE / Jean-Paul Hévin

HÉVIN, 46 years old, is ... nal star among choco- ... and pastry chefs, with ... ors and bars and cellars ... males in Tokyo, Rekuru, ... Yokohama. His products in- ... superfild with cheese, » a ... cheese and Roquefort cor- ... chocolate with spices and ... olate is a loudly preparing ... Chocolat, held from Oct. ...

makers were all going to Switzerland to study. Now students come from all over the world to learn how to make chocolate in France.

You have stopped imports to the U.S. for now, because of problems with the U.S. Customs Service. Yet other French chocolate makers like Bonnat and Michel Cluizel are still shipping to the States.

I haven't checked with other companies, but for the last four months, our shipments have been blocked for up to 12 days by U.S. Customs, after which we feel that the product is no longer good and cannot be sold. Our American customers complain a lot, but I can't do anything about it. One fellow complained to the Customs, who said, "What do you plan to do with this chocolate?" The customer said, "We want to eat it, that's all!" To no avail.

Christian Dior has developed a Chocolate Amer (Bitter Chocolate) lipstick, which will polish and enhance the lips in ... free from Givenchy, Chanel, Guerlain, Clarins, Clinique and Yves Saint Laurent are also chocolate-based. For me, these products are different from real chocolate, a chocolate perfume made synthetically does not really resemble the real smell of chocolate. The synthetic smell is not as refined as the original, which up to now I have found to be matchless.

Some chocolate makers claim that chocolate is good for the health, and makes us live longer, smarter and happier free—would you agree?

In moderate amounts chocolate offers all this, and above all it does no harm. There's a gentleman who lives in the Vosges Mountains, nearly 100 years old...

flavor which interests me in making chocolate. We have over 30 kinds of cocoa beans, each with its own specificity because the sun and the land are a certain way where it comes from—it's like wine. The cocoa beans ferment as they dry, then they are grilled in Europe and we can add sugar and milk, depending on what kind of chocolate we are making.

Does Switzerland deserve its reputation as Europe's great chocolate maker?

In Switzerland chocolate may be better loved than in France. The Swiss consume more milk chocolate than the French do. But in terms of sheer quality, Switzerland is less impressive now than in previous years. Its milk chocolate is more mass-produced than handmade. The only European country which has handmade chocolate today is France. Not even Belgium can say that. Belgian chocolate used to be better, although one or two...

...isn't a precise language to describe chocolate. We try to determine the taste of chocolate through color, taste and its specificity. Until now, the words haven't existed to describe these elements. So four years ago we formed the French Academy of Chocolate (académie française du chocolat) with forty members, just like the French Academy. We meet regularly in Paris, chocolate makers, engineers and researchers, all of us passionate about chocolate. We are establishing a dictionary of...

SA RECETTE EXPRESS

Crêpes au chocolat

Ingrédients pour 6 personnes
170 g de farine pâtissière, 85 g de sucre semoule, 2 œufs, 50 cl de lait, 70 g de beurre fondu.
Zeste de citron vert.
FINITION : tablette de chocolat noir à 72 % de cacao.

● Dans un saladier, mélanger les ingrédients les uns après les autres dans l'ordre. Lorsque la pâte est bien lisse, la laisser reposer à température ambiante une heure.
● Faire chauffer une crêpière ou une poêle antiadhésive et la graisser avec une noix de beurre frais. Une fois la poêle bien chaude, verser une louche de pâte, puis étaler.
● En fin de cuisson, à l'aide d'un Économe, disposer délicatement des copeaux de chocolat noir.
● Déposer les crêpes dans un plat et les couvrir si vous ne les servez pas tout de suite.
VARIANTE : Napper la crêpe d'une pâte à tartiner. Un pur moment de bonheur !

Jean-Paul HÉVIN

Chocolatier inventif, installé depuis près de vingt ans il a conquis la planète, de la France au Japon. Il nous propose une recette simple qui enchantera petits et grands.

Il déteste : manger...

Il aime : bien manger... et avec sa femme si possible

Son péché mignon : un thé accompagné d'un chou à la crème que J.-P. H. avec ses enfants

Son ingrédient indispensable : le chocolat pour sa couleur, son odeur, son goût, son énergie, sa complexité, ses mille saveurs

Ses fournisseurs préférés : François Pralus pour sa gentillesse, sa sincérité, la qualité de sa pâte de cacao et de ses produits. Stéphane de Luze pour la qualité exceptionnelle de ses bas-armagnacs et de ... « l'Amour des trois oranges... Mais aussi la maison Valrhona, les laiteries d'Échiré et bien d'autres fournisseurs soucieux de la qualité de leurs productions au quotidien.

Son plus : son mont-blanc servi tous les vendredis et samedis au salon de thé.

Par Frédérique Deder
Photos David Aslan

в гостях у сказки
что ест Дед Мороз
Олимпиада
кто увез медали
московские планы
Алана Дюкасса
...олный ...еский журнал
...рь 12/1 (23) 2004/05
...ОДЕЦ
...а блюде
...СЬЕ на ...ОКОЛАД
...рономический календарь на 2005 год

NIKITA ①知恵鏡

05

聖夜最後のカンパイは
アタクシと♥

Bûche Cube
...より/Complice
...Intense (白)、Fidelium
...ぐ5ぺ（2名で）、魅力的な全
...Intense)。￥27（4人分）

RECIPES
ADAPTED FROM
THE COLLECTION OF

Jean-Paul Hévin

Brownies

Serves 6

3/4 cup fresh butter
3 1/2 ounces chocolate (70% cocoa solids)
1/2 cup packed brown sugar
3 tablespoons fine granulated sugar
3 egg yolks

1/3 cup pastry flour
1 1/2 tablespoons cocoa powder
3 egg whites, beaten till foamy
2/3 cup (3 ounces) chopped pecans
A little softened butter to grease the pan

1. Preheat oven to 375°F. Grease a shallow rectangular or square pan.

2. Whisk together the butter and the chocolate, then the sugars and the egg yolks. Add the flour and the cocoa.

3. Fold in the beaten egg whites in three stages, then add the pecans. Mix lightly.

4. Bake at 375°F for 35 minutes.

5. Let cool to the touch before cutting and serving warm. Leftovers can be frozen.

Chocolate Cake

Serves 6–8

CAKE BATTER

5/8 cup softened butter
1 2/3 cups confectioners' (icing) sugar
5 tablespoons ground almonds
A few drops of vanilla
3 large eggs
1 2/3 cups sifted flour
3/4 teaspoon baking powder

1/2 cup cocoa powder
1 teaspoon ground cinnamon
1 teaspoon ground coriander
1 ounce thin chocolate wafers
(80% cocoa solids), chopped
A little softened butter to grease the pan

TOPPING

Brown rum

1. Preheat oven to 475°F. Grease a rectangular standard cake pan and line with parchment paper.

2. Prepare batter by mixing in a bowl the softened butter, confectioners' (icing) sugar, ground almonds, and vanilla. Slowly add eggs, flour, and baking powder. Without stirring, add cocoa, cinnamon, and coriander. Now stir 2 to 3 minutes, until well blended.

3. Stir in the chopped chocolate wafers.

4. Fill the prepared cake pan with batter.

5. Bake at 475°F for 9 minutes, then remove from the oven and gently split the top of the cake with a knife.

6. Return cake to oven, and bake for 50 minutes at 350°F or until a knife inserted in the center comes out clean.

7. Remove cake from oven, and drizzle lightly with brown rum.

8. Once cool to the touch, remove cake from pan and serve warm or cold. Cake will stay fresh for about four days, and can be wrapped in plastic food wrap and frozen.

Clafoutis

Serves 6

1 cup crème fraîche at room temperature
1/2 cup fine granulated sugar
3 eggs
Scant 1/2 cup pastry flour
1 ounce chocolate (70% cocoa solids),
chopped and melted
12 ounces (1 1/2 cups) pitted cherries
Pinch of salt

TOPPING
6 whole cherries
1 tablespoon toasted, slivered almonds

1. Preheat oven to 325°F. Whisk together the crème fraîche and the sugar. Add the eggs one at a time, and beat until well combined.

2. Gently stir in the flour and the salt, then add the melted chocolate (it should be very hot). Stir gently.

3. Distribute the pitted cherries evenly in 6 small ovenproof dishes or 1 large oven-proof dish. Pour the mixture over the cherries.

4. Bake at 325°F for 15 minutes (20 minutes for the large dish). Remove from the oven. Be careful not to overcook as it will thicken and lose desired delicate consistency. Let cool to the touch.

5. Garnish with whole cherries and toasted, slivered almonds. Serve warm.

Madeleinettes

Makes some 80 madeleinettes

1 cup (16 tablespoons) butter	1 1/2 tablespoons honey, warmed
7/8 cup pastry flour	3 1/2 ounces chocolate (80% cocoa solids),
2 cups confectioners' (icing) sugar	finely chopped
7/8 cup ground almonds	Zest of 3 oranges
8 egg whites, lightly beaten	Zest of 1 lemon

1. In a pot or skillet, melt the butter gently until it is a light brown color. Stop the cooking process by placing the pot into a cold water bath. Let sit.

2. Using a round-bottomed mixing bowl, mix the flour, sugar, and ground almonds. Then add the lightly beaten egg whites. Whisk the ingredients together.

3. Add the warm honey, the chopped chocolate pieces, and the orange and lemon zest, then pour into the batter the still slightly warm melted butter. Let sit 2 hours in the refrigerator.

4. Preheat oven to 350°F. Butter mini Madeleine molds.

5. Fill each prepared Madeleine mold using a pastry bag fitted with a No. 6 pastry tube.

6. Bake in the oven at 350°F for approximately 20 minutes.

Crunchy Chocolate Mousse

Makes eight glasses or eight, three-inch ramekins

3 fresh egg yolks
1/4 cup sugar, divided
1 1/2 cups whipping cream
3 1/2 tablespoon whole milk

4 ounce chocolate (70% cocoa solids), chopped
3/8 cup crunch mix (candy sprinkles,
macaroons, puffed rice, chopped and
caramelized almonds or hazelnuts, etc.)

1. In a bowl, beat the egg yolks and half the sugar with an electric beater until the mixture turns a pale yellow.

2. In a second bowl, whip the cream to a smooth consistency. Set aside.

3. Pour the milk and the remaining sugar into a pan. Bring to a boil and pour one third of the milk mixture over the egg yolk mixture. Stir, then pour the egg mixture into the pan and heat to 185°F, being careful not to overcook. Remove from heat.

4. Put chopped chocolate into a bowl and pour the milk and egg mixture over it; mix well to obtain a smooth, shiny ganache. Let cool to 125°F, then add a small amount of the whipped cream. Mix well.

5. Pour ganache over the remaining whipped cream and mix again.

6. Gently incorporate the crunch mix into the mousse, saving a few pieces for the topping. Using a pastry bag, fill eight glasses or eight, three-inch ramekins with the chocolate mousse and refrigerate 1 hour. Decorate with a few pieces of the crunch mix just before serving. The chocolate mousse is best eaten the same day.

VARIATION

To keep the crunch mix crisp, perform step six just before serving.

Pomponnettes

Makes 50 pomponnettes

1 pound almond paste
of equal parts sugar and almonds
5 fresh eggs
2/3 cup butter, melted

Zest of 1 lime
Nuts (walnuts, hazelnuts, etc.)
and/or candied fruits
(candied orange, amarena cherries, etc.)

1. Vigorously mix almond paste with the eggs using an electric beater. Once the mixture has whitened, add the melted butter and lime zest.

2. Refrigerate 1 hour.

3. Preheat oven to 350°F. Butter fifty, one-inch petit four molds.

4. Fill prepared molds using a pastry bag fitted with a No. 6 pastry tube and sprinkle nuts and/or candied fruits on top, as desired.

5. Bake for approximately 20 minutes at 350°F.

Chocolate Pot

Serves 6

2 cups fresh whole milk

2 tablespoons cocoa powder

3 eggs

1 egg white

Scant 2/3 cup fine granulated sugar

1/2 ounce chocolate (80% cocoa solids), chopped

1. Preheat oven to 275°F.

2. Heat milk and add the cocoa powder. Bring to a boil.

3. In a bowl, whisk the 3 eggs, the egg white, and the fine granulated sugar.

4. Pour the boiling milk over the egg mixture, whisk vigorously, and add the chocolate. Continue to whisk until well blended.

5. Pour mixture into 6 small ovenproof dishes. Bake in a water bath for 20 minutes. Remove from the oven, let cool, and serve at room temperature.

TIP

An exception in its category, the Chocolate Pot may be kept for two to three days in the refrigerator but should not be served cold.

Sherbets

Serves 6

COCOA SHERBET	RASPBERRY SHERBET	
1 2/3 cups water	2/3 cup water	2 tablespoons + 1 teaspoon
1 cup sugar	1 1/2 teaspoons invert sugar	lemon juice
1/3 cup cocoa powder	or honey	
3 1/2 ounces chocolate	5/8 cup sugar	COULIS (SAUCE)
(100% cocoa solids)	2 1/4 cups raspberry pulp	3/8 cup fruit pulp
	1 1/2 cups loosely packed	1 1/2 tablespoons sugar
	raspberries	1 1/2 tablespoons water

COCOA SHERBET

1. Bring the water and sugar to a boil. Remove from heat; 2. Stir in cocoa powder, and bring to a boil; 3. Stir in chocolate. Let the mixture cool; 4. Put mixture in an ice cream maker until it reaches the desired consistency; 5. Using an ice cream scoop, fill chilled cocktail glasses with the sherbet.

RASPBERRY SHERBET

1. Bring the water, invert sugar or honey, and sugar to a boil. Remove from heat; 2. Add the pulp, small pieces of raspberries, and lemon juice; 3. Put mixture in an ice cream maker until it reaches the desired consistency; 4. Using an ice cream scoop, fill chilled cocktail glasses with the sherbet. Top with coulis: bring fruit pulp, sugar, and water to a boil in a pan. Refrigerate, then drizzle over sherbet.

TIP

Prepare purees of seasonal fresh fruit and freeze. Thaw puree about three quarters of the way and use in place of the fruit pulp in the sherbet recipes.

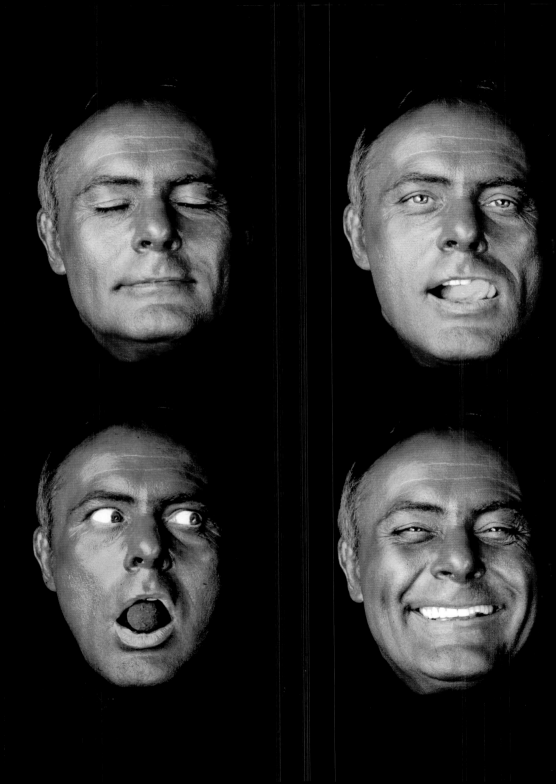

Chronology

1957: Jean-Paul Hévin is born in Méral, Mayenne, France.

1974: Earns a vocational certificate as pastry chef, chocolatier, and ice-cream maker.

1975: Apprentices as confectioner at the InterContinental Hotel, Paris.

1976–1988: Serves as apprentice confectioner, then pastry chef at the Hotel Nikko, Paris.

1979: Wins gold medal at the Concours Gastronomique in Arpajon, France.

1980: Wins first prize in the Charles Proust competition.

1983: Wins first prize at the French Pastry Cup, and in the Grand Prix International de la Chocolaterie.

1984: Wins first prize in the Vase de Sèvres, offered by the president of the French Republic at the Concours Gastronomique in Arpajon.

1984–1985: Works as head of the Peltier culinary laboratory in Tokyo, Japan.

1986: Wins the Meilleur Ouvrier de France (Best Craft Worker in France) award for pastry/confectionary.

1988: Opens his first shop, Le Petit Boulé, at 16 avenue de la Motte-Picquet, Paris.

1990: Opens a shop at 3 rue Vavin, Paris.

1997: Opens a shop/tea salon at 231 rue Saint-Honoré, Paris.

1999: Creates his own line of cheese-flavored chocolate appetizers.

2000: Creates his own line of chocolate energy bars.

2002: Le Petit Boulé moves to its new location at 23 bis de l'Avenue de la Motte-Picquet, Paris.
Opens two chocolate-themed bars and cellars in Tokyo and Hiroshima, Japan.
Opens the Hévin2 shop and releases a line of ready-to-eat chocolate.

2003: The Club des Croqueurs de Chocolat (Chocolate Crunchers Club) awards Jean-Paul Hévin a "five chocolate bar" rating in its ranking of French chocolate makers.

2004: Opens two chocolate-themed bars and cellars in Kokura and Hakata, Japan.
The financial daily newspaper *Nikkei Shinbun* ranks Jean-Paul Hévin the number one chocolate maker in Japan.

2005: June 1, the Jean-Paul Hévin chocolate macaroon is elected the best macaroon in Paris in the "traditional" category—a ranking confirmed five months later by *Le Figaroscope*.

2006: In February, Jean-Paul Hévin opens a new shop in the Omotesando Hills commercial center of Tokyo.
April 3, Flammarion publishes Jean-Paul Hévin's book, *Délices de Chocolat*.
October 5, Éditions Agnès Viénot publishes Jean-Paul Hévin's book, *Chocolat: 10 chocolats, 10 recettes en 10 minutes par un grand chef!* ("10 sur dix" collection).

2007: In March, opens a shop and a chocolate-themed bar in the Roppongi area of Tokyo.

"All chocolate" portrait of Jean-Paul Hévin. © Jean Cazals.

JEAN-PAUL HÉVIN

Chocolate Grinder (No. 1), Marcel Duchamp, 1913, oil on canvas, 27.2" x 25.4", Louise and Walter Arensberg collection (1950), The Philadelphia Museum of Art, Pennsylvania. © 2004. Photo The Philadelphia Museum of Art/Art Resource/Scala, Florence, © Marcel Duchamp Succession/ADAGP, Paris 2008.
"This iron spatula is sort of my fetish object. It's even a kind of messenger because it relays my desire and my intention to the chocolate. The chocolate interacts well with it, doesn't stick to it, and responds right away because it is dealing with a serious, solid material. Chocolate and iron (like marble) are the same family, a noble family." © Quentin Bertoux.

Extérieur de la boutique Jean-Paul Hévin au 231 de la rue Saint-Honoré, à Paris.
© Jean-Paul Hévin.

Jean-Paul Hévin in Brazil, in May 2007. "I try to come to Brazil as often as I can, to be closer to the planters and others involved in making cocoa. Nothing is more fragile because the cocoa beans have to be kept out of the sun and away from diseases. We practically have to hold [the producers'] hands to make them deliver their best. That's probably the best way to improve the quality of the cocoa." © Ayumi Shino.
Drying cocoa beans, in Brazil, May 2007. © Ayumi Shino.

Safi: "When I began to create this almond-based cocoa biscuit, filled with a bitter orange-chocolate mousse, I wanted to make something between a cake and a creamy chocolate mousse. I wanted to create a pastry that could be eaten from the hand like an éclair. My goal was this: an intermediary of textures." © Quentin Bertoux.
A pastry menu: (from top to bottom, left to right) *Chocolate Tart, Praline Longchamp, Praline Feuilletine, Safi, Choco Passion, Chocolate Millefeuille, Caracas, Ecuador, Turin, Bergam, Chocolate Raspberry, Cigar, Old-fashioned Macaroon, Marquise, Mont-Blanc,* and *Guayaquil.* © Quentin Bertoux.

Bilboquet, an Easter 2006 creation. "Where did I get the idea for the bilboquet? I don't know exactly. It must have come from my childhood and flowed through numerous cogitations. I spend days and nights looking without finding. And then one morning, without knowing how (so to speak), an idea appears." © Quentin Bertoux.
Cacao tree pods. © Jean-Paul Hévin.

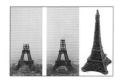

The construction of the Eiffel Tower seen from one of the towers of the Trocadéro Palace (October 14–November 4, 1888), anonymous, Musée d'Orsay, Paris. © René-Gabriel Ojéda/RMN.
"I made an Eiffel tower in chocolate because I saw [the real one] every day from my first shop. Mine was made with chocolate thread-like lace. I like the lightness of it. Sometimes when we create, we border on kitsch or misunderstanding, but this allusion pleases me. I keep it because it makes a statement." © Quentin Bertoux.

Chocolate laboratory, June 2007. "Making a ganache seems as easy as hitting a backhand in tennis. But it is very complex because you have to create a very smooth texture, a perfect virtuosity. So you have to play with the whisk, avoid air bubbles, modulate the speeds to obtain this small miracle. A ganache made this way is never the same as any other." © Ayumi Shino.

Harcourt mini-glass in chocolate, a Christmas 2006 creation. A Baccarat icon since its creation in 1841, the *Harcourt* Service is emblematic of the famous crystal glasshouse's unique skill. © Quentin Bertoux.

L'Oeuf à la coque (soft-boiled egg), André Beaudin, 1923, 31.9" x 21.6", Musée national d'Art moderne/Centre Georges Pompidou, Paris. © Philippe Migeat/CNAC/MNAN Dist. RMN © ADAGP, Paris 2008.

Compressed Egg, an Easter 2005 creation. "The idea of this egg was to reverse the traditional arrangement. Why hide the filling, when it is so beautiful? So, I reversed it like you'd turn a coat inside out. The lining is attractive, we shouldn't hide it." © Quentin Bertoux.

"This chocolate bread is a bit of a jest. Not at all like chocolate éclairs, the great classics of pastry. For me, there are no éclairs except in chocolate. When they're successful, they're an enchantment, with the sweet cream, not too firm, and very chocolaty. The cream puff pastry echoes the lightness and slight crustiness. In your mouth, it's an ongoing contrast, added to by the fondant topping." © Jean Cazals.

Chocolate éclairs, cream puff pastry filled with chocolate pastry cream. © Jean Cazals.

"If this hot chocolate met with such success in Japan, it's no doubt because the way it is made (beaten by hand) recalls the way green tea is prepared. The secret is not only in the gestures, the nobility of a craft, but it is also the air that is incorporated that oxygenates the chocolate and gives it, for just a few moments, its airiness. As though it had come close to the gods." © Jean Cazals.

Almonds and coffee beans. © Jean Cazals.

Chocolate tart: Almond shortbread crust topped with a bitter chocolate ganache, baked in the oven, and covered with a *ganache-miroir* (shiny ganache). "Another secret? For this chocolate tart I added chocolate to the crust. It gives acidity, awakens the taste. The rest flows naturally with that softness and the *ganache–miroir*, for which I learned the technique from Lucien Peltier, a guardian spirit of French pastry along with Gaston Lenotre." © Jean Cazals.

Boxes made of chocolate. © Jean Cazals.

Seafood Pyramid, an Easter 2006 creation. © Quentin Bertoux.

Compressed Christmas Tree, a Christmas 2004 creation. "I produced this idea after I made the egg compression. This tree is part of that continuity. It's clearly a reference to the work of the sculptor César. Add on top, pile up, it's a kind of childhood jingle, a refrain we never tire of." © Quentin Bertoux.

Elective Affinities, René Magritte, 1933, oil on canvas, 41 x 33 cm. Signed at upper right "Magritte." Private collection. © René Magritte picture library/ADAGP, Paris 2008.
The Multi-egg: "One day, a Friday morning, Sonia Rykiel asked me for a 'magnificent' egg for the coming Monday because she had to organize a photograph for the Club des Croqueurs de Chocolat (Chocolate Crunchers Club). So I had to make a unique egg. This friendly challenge was like a catharsis. On Monday, the egg was ready with its different sizes and colors. It still pleases me today when I look at it!" © Jean Cazals.

Paule Ka chocolate dress (detail at left), for the 11th Salon du Chocolat, in Paris, 2005. "It was three days from the opening of the Salon du Chocolat in Paris, and we had to find an idea associated with the world of the fashion designer Serge Cajfinger, founder of the Paule Ka house. The idea just came. The dress was a great success and made the journey to Tokyo. After which, it had a dignified end for a chocolate: It melted." © Vanessa Roy/Salon du Chocolat.

Chocolate Stiletto, a Christmas 2004 creation. "For his elegant magazine *Stiletto*, Laurence Benaïm came to see me and challenged me to make a model of a Rodolphe Menudier shoe. I adore this kind of challenge. The model surprised everyone, even me. Since then, it is one of the most spectacular assets of the stores." © Quentin Bertoux.

Bi-forme, Victor Vasarely, 1962, Saint-Gobin glass, metal, 78.7" x 47.2" x 7.8", Musée national d'Art moderne/Centre Georges Pompidou, Paris. © Philippe Migeat/CNAC/MNAM Dist. RMN, © ADAGP, Paris 2008.
Dark and milk chocolate lollipops: "Like with the bilboquet, this idea just came on its own. Well, almost. The lollipop is presented in a cardboard cube, and this association of the round and the square works naturally. Once it is in place, the model carries on its life all by itself." © Jean Cazals.

Compression, César (César Baldaccini), 1955, Hamburger Kunsthalle, Hamburg (Germany). © Hamburger Kunsthalle, Hamburg, Germany/The Bridgeman Art Library, © ADAGP, Paris 2008.
Compression Pascale, an Easter 2003 creation. "This compression is a tribute to César. It cost me a little to enter this domain of borrowing, but it rid me of my complexes, forced me to confront and move beyond my natural reserve. Admittedly it's copying a master, but by climbing on his shoulders." © Quentin Bertoux.

Assortment of macaroons. © Laziz Hamani.
Chocolate macaroon: "I have a passion for the macaroon because it belongs to the family of fugitives. It disappears in one bite. Catch it! I have always tried to make it lighter, less sweet: that's my battle." © Laziz Hamani.

The diversity of the Louvre: the Ieoh Min Pei pyramid (1988) along the axis of the Arc de Triomphe du Carrousel (built by Charles Percier and Pierre Fontaine in 1806) and the Sully wing. © Keiichi Tahara.
Pyramid: "This cocoa biscuit with almond paste, sprinkled with fresh pistachio nuts, filled with bitter ganache and a mild cognac flavored punch, is a tribute to the Louvre pyramid. This place fascinates me: I wanted to follow in its wake. The presence of the pistachio is a modern twist; it adds an unexpected touch." © Quentin Bertoux.

Caramels: "The caramel is the referent of childhood, always was, always will be. It combines a soft texture and an intense flavor; it is even ruthless in its expression: when we don't quite get it right, when it is not successful, it's immediately noticeable." © Laziz Hamani.
The chocolate spread: "In this creation inspired by Nutella, there is of course a whole dimension of childhood. That established, I wanted to go further, to give to adulthood the same cream with more depth, more intensity—to be able to say that we've progressed, that we've grown. Thinking about childhood is not necessarily regressive." © Laziz Hamani.

Please Touch, Marcel Duchamp, 1947, 16.4″ x 13.6″ x 2.7″, Musée national d'Art moderne/Centre Georges Pompidou, Paris. © Philippe Migeat/CNAC/MNAM Dist. RMN © Marcel Duchamp Succession/ADAGP, Paris 2008.
Le Sein Chocolat, a September 2007 creation. "I like the risk of starting from such a personal and intimate vision. This type of exercise suits me perfectly. It resembles me in spirit. I do it; then I keep quiet." © Quentin Bertoux.

International press tributes: (left-hand page, from top to bottom) *Madame Figaro* Taiwan, October 10, 2006; *Figaroscope,* March 28, 2007; *Version Femina,* January 28, 2007; *Le Figaro,* November 5–6, 2005; and *Elle,* October 30, 2006; (right-hand page, from top to bottom) *CREA Traveller,* November 28, 2006; *L'Express,* March 14, 2005; *Nikita,* October 7, 2006; *Jasmin,* February 5, 2007; *The Wall Street Journal,* October 2003; *Chef,* December 2004–January 2005; and *Point de Vue,* February 14, 2007.

International press tributes: (left-hand page, from top to bottom) *Madame Figaro* Taiwan, October 10, 2006; *Figaroscope,* March 28, 2007; *Version Femina,* January 28, 2007; *Le Figaro,* November 5–6, 2005; and *Elle,* October 30, 2006; (right-hand page, from top to bottom) *CREA Traveller,* November 28, 2006; *L'Express,* March 14, 2005; *Nikita,* October 7, 2006; *Jasmin,* February 5, 2007; *The Wall Street Journal,* October 2003; *Chef,* December 2004–January 2005; and *Point de Vue,* February 14, 2007.

Acknowledgments

A passion for taste took hold of me for no particular reason
and determined my life and my career.

I would particularly like to thank the people who supported me in this gourmet adventure.
First, those who trained me: M. Goupil at EPMT, Laval; Michel Foussard, winner of the
Meilleur Ouvrier de France, pastry section; and my great teacher, Joël Robuchon,
Meilleur Ouvrier de France, chef.
Second, all those who work with me: Alain Gabrielli, architect; Nathalie Georges with her
sharp eye for packaging; Jean Oddes, the artist and director; Quentin Bertoux, a photog-
rapher-magician; Lisa Kajita, public relations; Tristan de Pontevès, buyer; Virginie
Lamy, who possesses the appeal of marketing; Jean-Michel Bougrain, talented chocolate
chef, and his faithful assistant, Alexandre Verrier; Antoine Pabois, pastry chef; Chantal
Chibane, loyal manager of the Motte Picquet store and her assistant, Maï (15 years with
the firm); Émilie Calamotte, invaluable manager of the Saint-Honoré store; Olivia Hévin,
manager of the Vavin store; and Dany Morjat, manager of the Hévin2 store.
Finally, thanks to Brigitte Bury of Baccarat, Pascale Brun d'Arre of Paris Musées,
and Akemi Endo of JPH Japan public relations.
Many thanks to François Simon for lending me his pen.

I dedicate this book to my mother with much affection.

JEAN-PAUL HÉVIN

The editor would like to thank the photographers Quentin Bertoux, Jean Cazals,
Laziz Hamani, Vanessa Roy, Ayumi Shino and Keiichi Tahara, as well as Valentina
Bandelloni (Scala), Karine Caillieret (IMM Bruxelles), Py Cha, Laurence Doumenc
(The Bridgeman Art Library), Véronique Garrigues (ADAGP), Laurence Kersuzan
and Pierrick Jan (RMN), and Lara Streck.